Notes on Water

the poetry business

Published 2022 by
Smith|Doorstop Books
The Poetry Business
Campo House,
54 Campo Lane,
Sheffield S1 2EG

Copyright © Amanda Dalton 2022
All Rights Reserved

ISBN 978-1-914914-16-4
eBook ISBN 978-1-914914-17-1
Typeset by The Poetry Business
Printed by Biddles, Sheffield

Thanks to all the friends who gave me their watery stories and thoughts, some of which appear in one of these poems.

Smith|Doorstop Books are a member of Inpress:
www.inpressbooks.co.uk

Distributed by IPS UK, 1 Deltic Avenue,
Rooksley, Milton Keynes MK13 8LD

The Poetry Business gratefully acknowledges the support of Arts Council England.

Notes on Water
Amanda Dalton

smith|doorstop

Notes on Water

I'm swimming in an artificial pool
inside a broken building.
The water is deep and brown
and full of wreckage:
a floating rusted can, papers
swelling as they soak.
I'm out of my depth, weak
breaststroke turning to doggy paddle,
an ache in the shoulders and hips.

A pink balloon taps my face,
a flotilla of paper party cups, nothing
that will make a raft.
Beyond the water, flaked plaster,
smashed windows. Wires hang
from the walls. My sister
is kneeling in the rubble. She has
no idea how close I am to drowning.

>*Because of what happened,* he said, *when I think
>of rivers I can only remember the current's strength,
>how I never really reckoned with its power.*

>*The water was opaque. I'd no idea
>which way was up,* she said. *Or down.*

At 3am I wake thinking of the man
who will leave in winter. My gut is tight,
my head white noise. I'm dry.
I feel my way downstairs, fill the kettle

in the dark, not ready for electric light.
The water's force surprises me,
splashing the tiles, soaking my arm.
My feet ache on the slabs and I wonder
how anyone bears the cold of swimming
a freezing river, the going-in, the shock
on the belly, the whole body gasping.
I want to try it, want to see if it stops
my heart or snaps me wide awake.

*Stones in her pockets. I haven't read
her books but I know she drowned.*

*

Today there's a smiling boy in the car park,
little Noah, pouring rivers from a watering can.
He calls me out to see how his streams
gather speed as they make their way
down the sloping tarmac, forking as they catch
on grit. He starts another and another,
wills them to connect, thrills when they do.
I refill can after can and join him,
building settlements of broken stone.
Some become islands, some are flooded,
some survive the bursting riverbanks.
He builds a shop and we plan to make the islanders
a boat but Ben is driving away in a van
and he can't help it – he's flattening the houses,
everything is smeared and re-routed when he's gone.

*By lunchtime all roads in and out were blocked.
And I realised we were cut off, completely.*

I'm seven on a beach in Wales,
crying as the tide stalks
my mountain range of sand,
its rivulets of seawater, its waterfalls,
the valley town at its base with a river,
farmstead, fields.
Dad said it would be prone to flooding
and it is. I rescue my plastic animals,
leave the world to drown.

> *It wasn't drowned,* they said. *It was flooded.*
> *'Drowned's a soft word. Nothing soft in this,*
> *except for the stinking mud.*

> *The Calder, Colden, Hebden Water, all in town.*
> *I hate that river.*
> *Which one?*
> *The one that was in my house.*

The one that made the whole town one big filthy river; floating cars on Albert Street, St George's Square an artificial lake, a drunken slap on a cheek, and the soaking books in supermarket trolleys, toxic slime on shovels, shoes, between the floorboards, up the walls. The drenched and the nowhere-to-go and the lost-the-lot and don't say it's almost beautiful the way the burst banks re-made the woods, don't say that a flooded cinema's romantic. So many carpets on the pavements. So many fridges, sofas, Christmas trees. Open the door and the hall's in the cellar, open the door and the TV's caked in slime. There's a man in tears in the road with his dog on his shoulders, looking at his half-submerged front door. Next day the fucking sightseers blocking the streets.

Next day the water sings. I walk the bank
with someone else's dog on a lead.
And it's like the river's saying *Yes?*
An ordinary day. Nothing doing here.
I watch a wagtail wagging stone to stone,
even the living-statue heron's there,
powdered grey, and I ask the dog
if we should give it a coin for its trouble.
There's a sycamore down and some branches
on the path but nothing like the fallen army
ripped apart that day in Ardnamurchan,
that defeated battlefield of trees
enough to make you weep. Then the dog
says *flow* and I say *fucking hippy dog*
and the river says
I'm thinking of the man who will leave in winter.

I am thinking of David Nash's *Wooden Boulder*,
that great ball of oak, slipping downstream,
stuttering for months, coming to rest
in the estuary until the heavy rains, high tides,
dislodge it again and again and it's gone.
I am thinking of David Nash gently searching
for years, how he said *It hasn't vanished.*
I just can't see it.

And the dog says *That'll do. Think that.*
Hasn't disappeared. You just can't see it.

*

On the far side of the artificial pool
my sister is kneeling in the rubble

talking to an empty window frame,
talking to the wire that hangs from the wall,
telling the tale of a woman who walked her dog
beside a river that was fast and high.

The dog jumped in my sister tells the window frame,
*was swept away. The woman followed the river
for miles, running and driving and shouting
for strangers to help her search for the dog
but no-one found it, ever.*

Lighten up, I say to my sister, mouth full
of rusty water, grasping a paper party cup,
a pink balloon.

> *I remember walking and driving
> near the River Wye*, he said.
> *Never quite knowing where it would turn up next.*

> *I love that the stream by my house,* she said,
> *runs to the Calder which joins the Ouse
> which passes my brother's, becomes the Humber
> which goes by Mum and Dad's.*

> *Never mind that saying,* he said. *That saying
> 'you can't step into the same river twice'.
> If I follow the river at its rate of travel,
> the water I sample at the confluence might
> include the water I sampled at the source!*

I'm beside it, drinking beer, the river,
sunlight popping, rocks gargling,
even the knot of flies at the bridge is beautiful.

I want to jump into the water, feel its liquid
rush, but I'm busy looking at maps to calculate
how long it would take for this particular stretch
to reach the man who will leave in winter.
And the answer is *forever* or, more brutally,
is *never*. The Calder joins the Aire at Castleford,
flows to the start of the Humber. *Useless.*
Derwent joined by the Wye at Rowsley – *Stop!*
This is stupid, pointless, childish, rather difficult.
Drink beer. Drift.

>*No, no,* she said, *it's not the meandering drift.*
>*What I love about rivers is SYSTEMS.*
>*That's in capital letters because it matters!*
>*Rivers are the circulation system of the land!*

*

There's an iPad on the floor of the broken building.
A YouTube man is teaching my sister to dance.

>*Start with your right foot,* he says, *in front of your left.*
>*We're gonna hop on our left foot and then place down*
>*our right.*
>
>*Hop.   1. Pick up the left foot* (and he's hopping)
>*place it down for two.   2. Pick up the right in front—*

and my sister is up on her feet, stepping and hopping and laughing
and I laugh too and whatever she's doing looks nothing
like a river dance.

Then this.
This – before I have said goodbye to the man
who will leave in winter, before I can write
of the tall church spire that protrudes
from the lake in a drought, before I remember
the water diviner who found the line of liquid,
pure and running white beneath the old school hall.
This.

How to describe it?

A fault line that appeared in the ground in an instant,
patterned not unlike a river bed and running fast
as Noah's little rivers, veining, widening, but dry as a bone?

A breach? Rubble falling down the gaps, a crack
that might have been a gun shot, fog of dust
from walls that crumble silently?

I thought of the hotel that fell into the sea,
of the crockery and napkin rings still buried in the hill,
the floating coat hangers, the reading spectacles
a guest forgot to pack in his haste.

I thought of the terrific speed of the fall.

And as the pool fractured and the water
drained away, I thought of the stupid times
I'd stayed in the bath after pulling the plug,
the heaviness in the limbs, the little shiver,
and I lay on stone with the paper cups and the pink
balloon, my gut tight, head white noise. Dry.

And I knew I must go deeper, close my eyes
and drop through the cleft.
I knew I must find a river in the dark.

> *Hans was not mistaken*, he said,
> *in* Journey to the Centre of the Earth.
> *What you hear is the rushing of a torrent.*
> *– A torrent?*
> *There can be no doubt; a subterranean river*
> *flows around us.*

The water's force surprises me.
I go deep into it, wear it,
feel the weight lighten me.
I think I am in the river Cocytus
or maybe this is just black water
running underneath an urban street.

Somewhere far above my sister kneels,
drawing symbols in the dust
and the man who will leave in winter
slowly walks, a forked twig in his hands.
He knows what it takes to daylight a river
that runs underground; I know he is dowsing
for me. Soon he will find a stream
and follow it but

> *Stop! This is pointless. Some rivers never meet.*

He reaches the sea.

*

Down here is jackdaw black,
blacker than blackout, blacker
than Vantablack and I am
a cave fish, accidental troglomorph,
with nothing but a raft of papers
breaking down in the wet.
I circle counter-clockwise, swim
until the fragments of my skull
change shape and I'm asymmetrical,
losing colour, and my eyes are weak.

Time slows in the black, folds in
on itself and disappears or perhaps
it's only time that's moving me.
I navigate by touch. I barely eat
but still I feel these fins grow large
and though I can't see a thing
through these useless eyes,
they open and I wake.

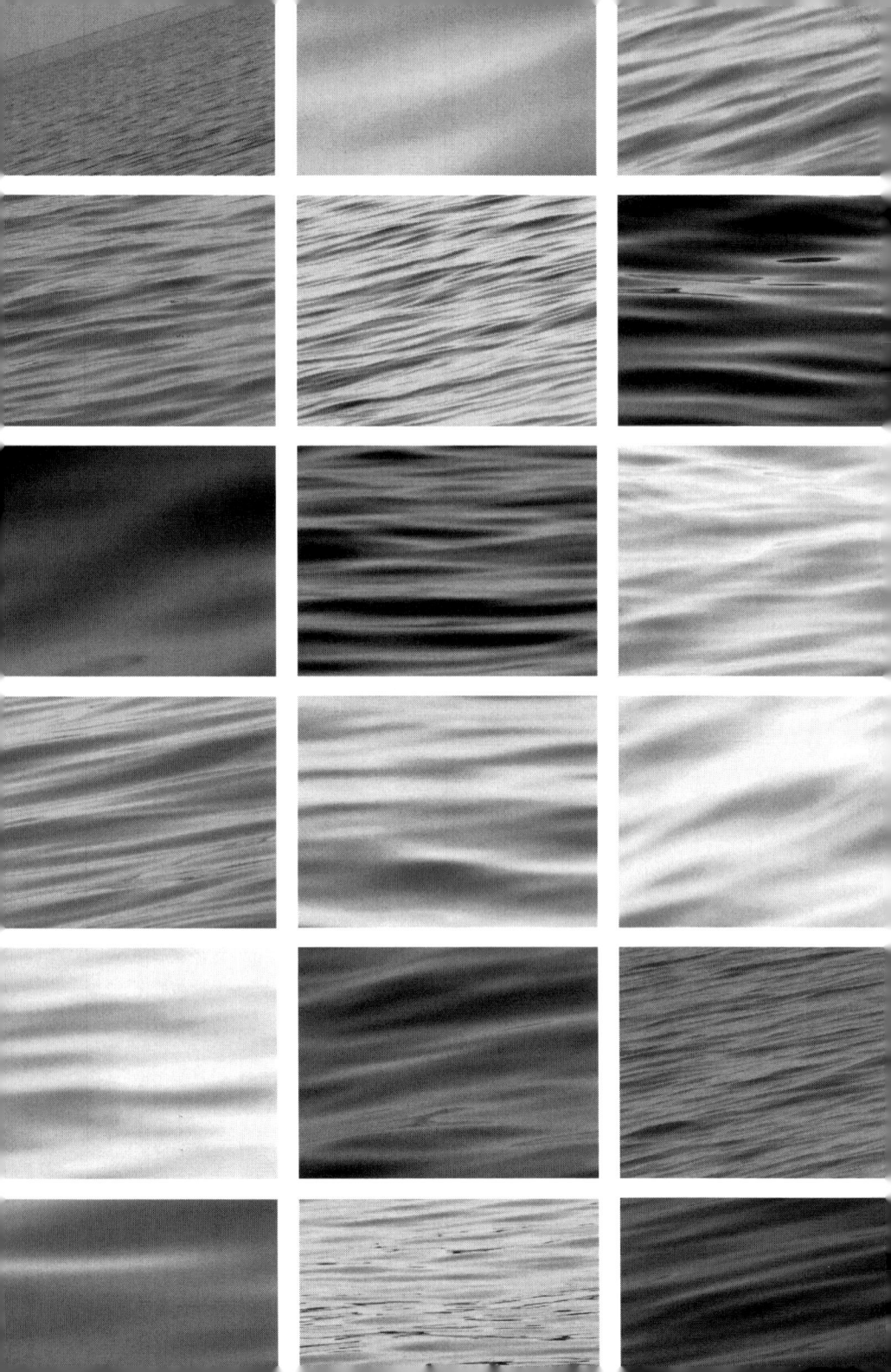

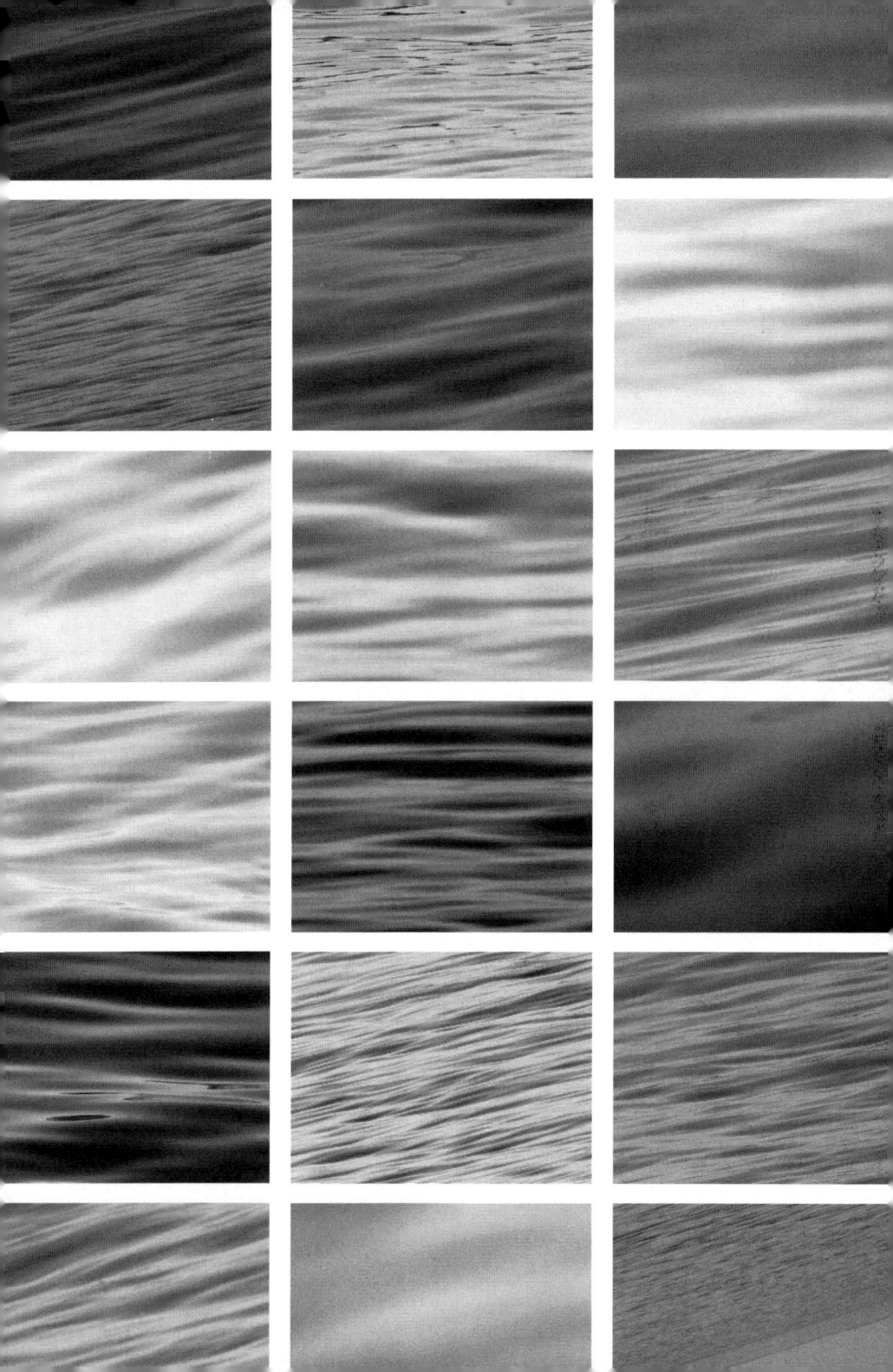

and swimming, in a fractured pool
in the bowels of an abandoned building.
Broken windows, rusted pipes. She's flailing,
breaststroke weak, can't see a thing,
but somehow, somehow she doesn't drown,
she wakes.

She's out with the rest of the town in wellies,
rubber gloves, remembering the last flood –
how he'd cursed his lack of strength to bail and lift,
how he'd driven instead, delivered food to homes
that were drowned and she knows she should be glad
he isn't seeing this.

Next day she walks the woods but her old path
is gone. Perhaps that's why she turns for home,
makes a list of everything she's shifted since he died,
imagines him coming back to the tidy house:
new doorbell, missing folders, mended light.
Would she run from room to room like an excited child,
show him what she's rearranged? Or apologise?

*

She waits for his car headlights,
shadow on the steps, key in the door.
She waits for his ghost,
(though she's not sure she believes
in ghosts), waits at least to dream of him
alive. But nothing comes.
She chips a tooth, the car breaks down,
the cats bring a dead wood pigeon in,
the cellar floor is soaked, invoices fall
through the door, she watches the news –
half the world underwater, the rest in flame.

She dreams of strangers talking to her
but she can't hear what they say,
dreams of shrouded cityscapes and faces
lost in fog, dreams she's almost blind

thinks perhaps she had wanted to bathe his body
before they took it away, or is this a kind of
saying goodbye – to the smell of him,
to his skin, making sure he's no longer
there before she parts with him?
She hangs trousers, jumpers, jackets, shirts
on radiators, over rails, from the tops of doors,
until everywhere she turns, she sees him
all at once on different days, him
in a Pennine snowstorm, him in the blazing heat
of southern Spain. He stands behind her,
beside her, in front of a bookshelf, suddenly there
up close and she wants to bury her head
in his damp blue shirt but there's no chest
or shoulder and his arms are limp
and she can't tell is she taunted by the way that
everything hangs in his shape
those weeks before he died – so thin,
too weak for an embrace and she's overwhelmed
by his presence and by the absence of him.

*

A restless night, a storm, the threat of flood.
At 8am the ghostly wail of the siren and by midday
streets are flowing, steep roads surge.
Everything is river and the river is more than itself,
carrying vehicles on its back, a fallen tree, trying to
drag its feet to calm the rage but it's too headstrong,
churning silt and gravel, spewing up a pushchair,
plastic shoe, dead jackdaw, bin. Everything is brown
and broken. Everything is wet.

to tiny fruits
to water
on a spoon
to this –
the last of the nights and days
when she holds his parched hand,
moistens his lips with balm, cups
a tiny glass to him
but he chokes on a sip
and the beautiful nurse says
just a drop on the tongue, like this
and when he opens his mouth for her fingertip
he's a fledgling.

*

His feet are cold but he can't bear
the duvet, even a sheet, and so she looks
for socks and finds the swimming shorts
he never wore and never will.
(After he dies she can't quite part with them.)

He always said he hated swimming,
still he would dive into pools and she remembers
the violence of his splash, the wild front crawl,
the way he shot underwater, up and out
in a single breath.

*

Months after he dies she washes
his clothes by hand, has no idea why,

and she took photographs for him –

the wader she couldn't identify

the perfect reflection of a sheep

the evening light on the loch after rain

the view from the opposite shore

and she saw how they didn't interest him,
how they all looked the same.

*

These days she can't bear the sting
of the shower so she lies in the bath
for hours, lets water out, refreshes it
with hot until she scalds.
She thinks of how the wetness makes
her fingers look like his, the puckered
contours, knuckles pouched, but when
she touches her thumb to her middle finger
she hears a squelch, liquid moving
under her flesh.
And she wonders how half his body is water,
even now as he desiccates.

*

In just seven weeks he goes
from coffee and wine
to peppermint tea

even then? The start of a mass in his gut?
A stain? Did he feel dis-ease as it pooled
in his blood? Or was it later, on Ardnamurchan,
driving through pouring rain,
the day he slipped and fell in a storm of magnolia

blossom strewn like confetti on the muddy bank?
The day the deluge blocked the well and she searched
for buckets, found the brook, the bottled water,
laughed because this really didn't matter –
then saw how he couldn't cope anymore.

Later she'd walked alone by the sea loch, felt
the slow drip of loss. She wonders was that why
she made a list of everything she saw – to give
to him, to keep something from seeping away.

'bladderwort,' she wrote,
'white driftwood'
'flowers that might be meadow cranesbill'
'bits of wood.'

She couldn't stop—

'a Tennant's lager can, marsh marigold in clumps, 8 oystercatchers, 14
adult sheep, 9 lambs, a broken rowing boat, a pair of dark-coloured
ducks with 6 young, a crow, ringed plovers (5), red plastic – might be
from a child's spade, dead crab, a herring gull, sheep's wool, the remains
of a fire, 4 black-headed gulls, a plastic shoe (green), campion, plastic
bottles (3), seawort, marram grass, a length of rusted metal chain,
thousands of stones, 2 plastic bags, some shells, a rock, an orange rope,
moss, gorse, wet grass (muddy), rock samphire, blue plastic piping,
a broken pint glass (partly buried), sudden gathering of terns, a lot
of seaweed – mainly knotted wrack and kelp, gritty sand, a gang of
Canada geese, unexpected, round a bend'

Notes on Water

In a small terraced house
a woman waits through a long night.
She boils a kettle, washes cups,
palms three tangerines
to see if she remembers how to juggle.

The living room's reflected in the yard –
a sideboard hovers on the tiny pond,
her piano juts across the lane.
She's out there too, standing in the hedge,
wonders is it her ghost that waits inside.

Upstairs he lies soaked in pain
but still the doctor doesn't come.
2am. 4.30. 5.15. She phones again –
a busy night, they say. *They're on their way.*
She goes upstairs to sit with him

but it's easier to look at a photograph –
the one she'll decide to frame when he dies.
He's on a boat, all smiles, binoculars
around his neck, everything blue
and calm and bright.

That was the day they saw the dolphins
who surfaced, laughing, glided beside them
close enough to touch. A day
of unexpected Highland sun,
a kind of happiness – was it there

Notes on Water
Amanda Dalton

smith|doorstop

the poetry business

Published 2022 by
Smith|Doorstop Books
The Poetry Business
Campo House,
54 Campo Lane,
Sheffield S1 2EG

Copyright © Amanda Dalton 2022
All Rights Reserved

ISBN 978-1-914914-16-4
eBook ISBN 978-1-914914-17-1
Typeset by The Poetry Business
Printed by Biddles, Sheffield

Thanks to all the friends who gave me their watery stories and thoughts,
some of which appear in one of these poems.

Smith|Doorstop Books are a member of Inpress:
www.inpressbooks.co.uk

Distributed by IPS UK, 1 Deltic Avenue,
Rooksley, Milton Keynes MK13 8LD

The Poetry Business gratefully acknowledges
the support of Arts Council England.

Supported using public funding by

**ARTS COUNCIL
ENGLAND**

Notes on Water

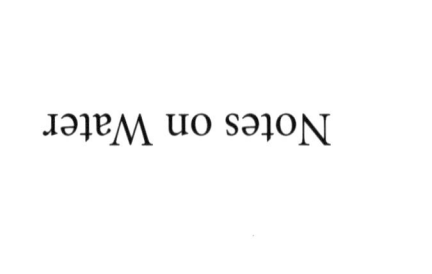